CODE READER™

Making Difficult Words Easy

Code Reader Books provide codes with "sound keys" to help read difficult words. For example, a word that may be difficult to read is "unicorn," so it might be followed by a code like this: unicorn *(YOO-nih-korn)*. By providing codes with phonetic sound keys, Code Reader Books make reading easier and more enjoyable.

Examples of Code Reader™ Keys

Long a sound (as in make):
a *(with a silent e)* or **ay**
Examples: able *(AY-bul)*; break *(brake)*

Short i sound (as in sit): **i** or **ih**
Examples: myth *(mith)*; mission *(MIH-shun)*

Long i sound (as in by):
i *(with a silent e)* or **y**
Examples: might *(mite)*; bicycle *(BY-sih-kul)*

Keys for the long o sound (as in hope):
o *(with a silent e)* or **oh**
Examples: molten *(MOLE-ten)*; ocean *(OH-shen)*

Codes use dashes between syllables *(SIH-luh-buls)*, and stressed syllables have capital letters.

To see more Code Reader sound keys, see page 42.

Strange Creatures

(KREE-churz)

TREASURE BAY

Strange Creatures

A Code Reader™ Chapter Book
Green Series

This book was created by Reimagined Classroom under agreement with Treasure Bay, Inc.

With special thanks to Emma Kocina,
biologist at the California Academy of Sciences,
for her review of the information in this book

Published by
Treasure Bay, Inc.
PO Box 519
Roseville, CA 95661 USA

Printed in China

Library of Congress Control Number: 2024944967

ISBN: 978-1-60115-730-0

Visit us online at:
CodeReader.org

PR-1-25

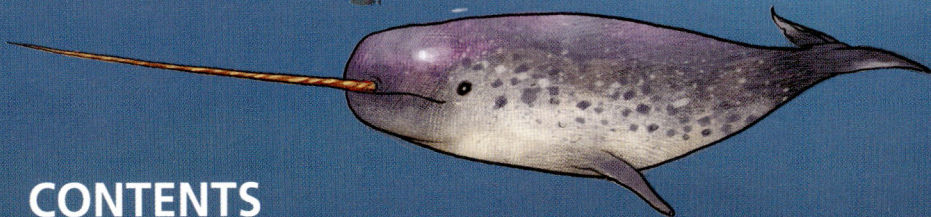

CONTENTS

Poison Dart Frog

Poison dart frogs are one of the world's most toxic, or poisonous *(POY-zuh-nuhs)*, animals! They are brightly colored and very tiny.

1 inch

Most poison dart frogs are only 0.5–1.5 inches long.

They live in rainforests in Central *(SEN-trul)* and South America. They like warm, tropical *(TRAH-pih-kul)* habitats.

habitat: the home of an animal that has the things it needs to live

Their bright colors
warn other animals
not to eat them because
they are toxic.

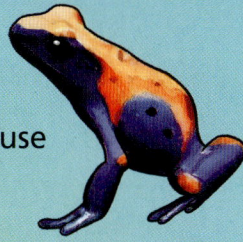

Warning:
Poisonous!

toxic: harmful or
poisonous

They can live for 3–15 years.
Poison dart frogs are
INSECTIVORES
(in-SEK-tuh-vorz).
They use their long, sticky
tongues *(tungz)* to catch flies
and other small bugs.

3

Komodo Dragon

The **Komodo dragon** *(kuh-MOH-doh DRAG-un)* is known as the "king of the lizards."

They are the largest and heaviest *(HEV-ee-est)* lizards in the world!

Komodo dragons can grow over 9 feet long and weigh *(way)* 150–250 pounds.

9 ft

Komodo Island *(I-lund)*

They live in Indonesia *(in-doh-NEE-zhuh)*, with the biggest group living on Komodo Island.

900 ft

Their ability to see things that are far away is awesome *(AW-sum)*! They can see things up to 900 feet away.

Komodo dragons are

CARNIVORES

(KAR-nih-vorz).
They use their forked tongues *(tungz)* to smell prey *(pray)*, as they hunt.

If they choose *(chooz)* to, they can run very quickly: up to 13 miles per hour.

Flying Snake

Flying snakes live in Southeast Asia *(AY-zhuh)*. They can be found in jungles *(JUNG-guls)* and forests. They range from 2–4 feet long. They are green, brown, red, or yellow. These colors help them blend in with their environment *(en-VY-urn-ment)*.

environment *(en-VY-urn-ment)*: the area *(AIR-ree-uh)* where a person, plant, or animal lives

Flying snakes can climb *(klime)* vertically, or straight *(strate)* up, trees.

When they decide to fly to another location *(loh-KAY-shun)*, they form a "C" or "J" shape with their bodies, flatten much of their body, and jump!

These snakes can fly or glide up to 300 feet. That is the length *(langth)* of a football field *(feeld)*!

300 ft

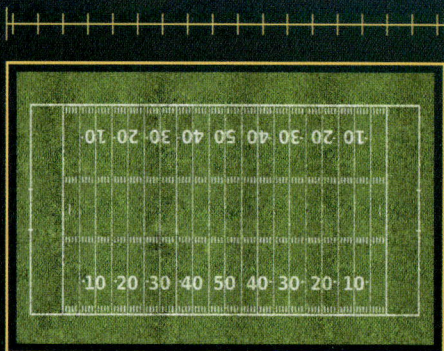

Blobfish

Blobfish are nicknamed the "world's ugliest fish." They live four thousand feet below the ocean's *(OH-shunz)* surface.

The blobfish has a big head and jelly-like body.

A BLOBFISH CAN LIVE TO BE 130 YEARS OLD!

High pressure *(PREH-shur)* deep in the ocean keeps the blobfish in a more fish-like shape. At the surface, the blobfish collapses into a blob-like shape.

It's a good thing the blobfish does not have predators *(PREH-dih-turz)* chasing it, because it is a very slow-swimming fish. To eat, they wait for prey like crabs and shrimp to sink, sniffing them out with their big flabby noses.

Blobfish Habitat

WORLD'S UGLIEST FISH!

Anglerfish

ANGLERFISH ARE CARNIVORES!

carnivore *(KAR-nih-vor)*: an animal that eats other animals

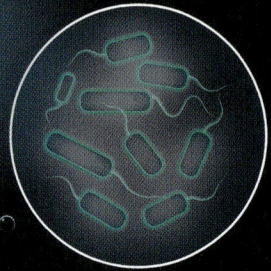

glowing bacteria *(bak-TEER-ee-uh)*

Anglerfish are *BONY (BOH-nee)* fish. Females *(FEE-mails)* have something called an **esca** *(ES-cuh)* that sticks out from their heads and lights up. The tiny bacteria *(bak-TEER-ee-uh)* that live in this organ make it GLOW.

Over 200 species *(SPEE-sheez)* of anglerfish live in the world's oceans. Most live at least a mile below the surface of the Atlantic and Southern Oceans.

Atlantic Ocean

Southern Ocean

Anglerfish Habitat

Some anglerfish are a few inches long. Others are 3.5 feet long.

|←+++++++++→| |←++++++++++++++++++++++++++++++→|

3.5 in.   **3.5 ft**

Anglerfish live in the deep, dark ocean. The glowing esca attracts **prey** like a fishing lure *(loor)*.

prey *(pray)*: an animal that is hunted and eaten by another animal

Colossal Squid

The **colossal** *(kuh-LAH-sul)* **squid** *(skwid)* is the most massive *(MAS-siv)* type of squid and probably the largest **invertebrate** *(in-VUR-teh-bret)* in the world!

invertebrate
(in-VUR-teh-bret): an animal that does not have a backbone

43 ft.

They have the biggest eyes of any animal. Each eye is the size of a soccer ball!

They also have very large pupils *(PYOO-puls)* that let them collect all of the light they can in the very deep, dark part of the ocean where they live.

A **colossal squid** can grow to be 43 feet long and weigh up to 1,500 pounds.

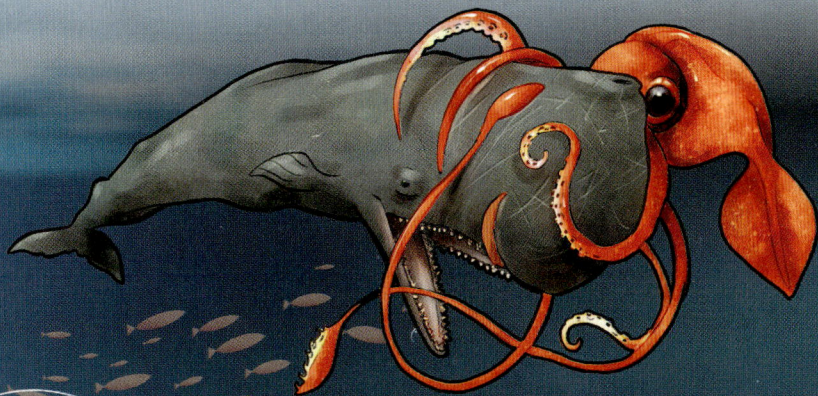

Sperm whales like to eat colossal squid, but the squid can try to escape or fight the whale.

Colossal squid live in the Southern Ocean, near Antarctica *(an-TARK-tih-kuh)*. Scientists *(SY-en-tists)* think they live 3,500–7,500 feet below the ocean's surface.

Their **tentacles** *(TEN-tuh-kulz)* have hooks on them that help them catch their prey.

Narwhal

In the icy waters of the Arctic Circle *(SUR-kul)* are animals nicknamed the "Unicorn *(YOO-nih-korn)* of the Sea" —the **narwhal** *(NAR-wol)*!

This air-breathing marine *(mah-REEN)* mammal is a type of toothed whale with black-brown markings on white skin.

18 ft.   **2,500 pounds**

Arctic Ocean

Found near the Arctic Circle

They live around 50 years, growing up to 18 feet and weighing *(WAY-ing)* up to 2,500 pounds—the weight of a small car!

They are most known for the tusk that grows on the males. This hollow spiral *(SPY-rul)* tusk is really a tooth and can grow almost 10 feet long!

Narwhals' predators are polar bears and orcas *(OR-kuhs)*.

Like other whales, narwhals make click and whistle *(WIH-sul)* sounds from their blowhole to communicate *(kuh-MYOO-nih-kate)*.

They also hunt with echolocation *(EH-coh-loh-KAY-shun)*, which is using *(YOO-zing)* sound echoes *(EH-koze)* to locate things.

Narwhals eat mostly Arctic cod and can dive up to 5,000 feet to hunt.

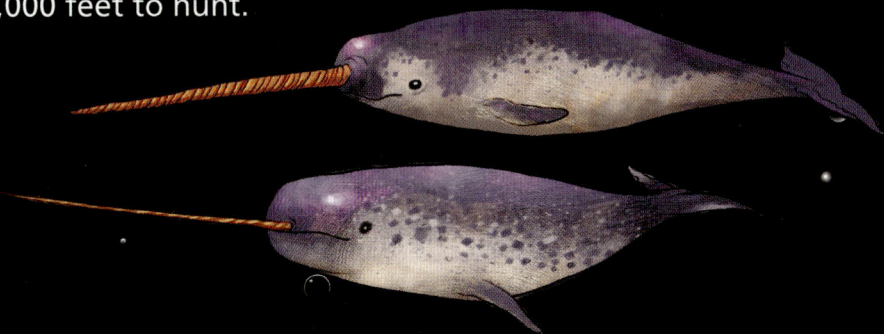

Narwhals travel together in pods of 5–20. They have seasonal *(SEE-zuh-nul)* migrations *(my-GRAY-shunz)*. In the summer months, pods can grow as large as 1,000 narwhals!

Black Sea Cucumber

The **black sea cucumber** *(KYOO-kum-bur)* is a very poisonous *(POY-zuh-nus)* type of sea cucumber.

If something brushes against it, the black sea cucumber will release a red fluid to scare away predators. When it is attacked, it shoots out a sticky, white poisonous liquid *(LIH-kwid)* from its body.

> **poisonous:** full of a dangerous *(DAYN-jer-us)* or harmful substance

Black sea cucumbers live in warm, shallow ocean waters. They live on reefs and use the tentacles around their mouths to find small animals and algae *(AL-jee)* to eat.

Fried Egg Jellyfish

Fried egg jellyfish are large! The bell—the circular (SUR-kyoo-lur) part on top—can grow up to 2 feet wide. Their tentacles can grow to be 10–30 feet long!

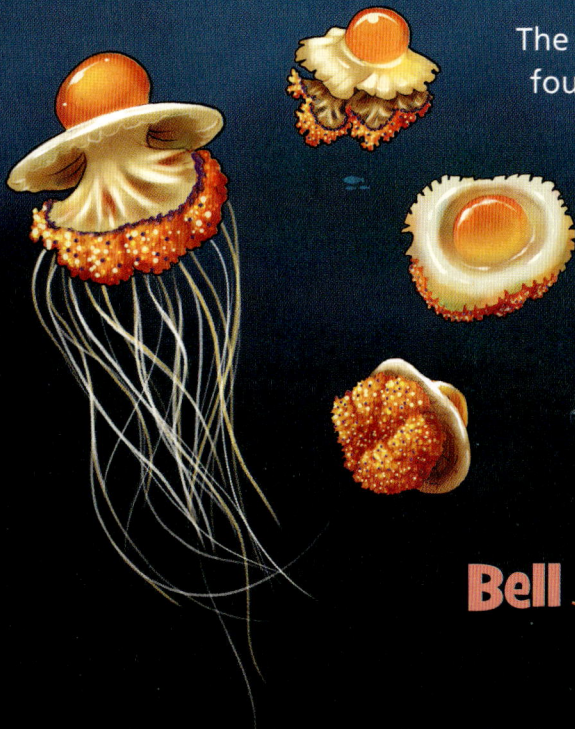

Mediterranean Sea

Pacific Ocean

Atlantic Ocean

The **fried egg jellyfish** can be found in the Mediterranean (meh-dih-tur-AY-nee-an) Sea and the Atlantic and Pacific (puh-SIF-ik) Oceans.

They can pulse (puls) their bodies to move, but they like to stay still and float in the water due to their large size.

Bell

They have a mild sting if attacked. Sometimes small animals, like crabs, ride on top of the jellyfish's bell as they float through the ocean.

Upside-Down Jellyfish

Upside-down jellyfish spend their days with their bells, or heads, flat on the ocean floor and their tentacles *(TEN-tuh-kulz)* moving *(MOOV-ing)* around.

They pulse their bodies to move in the water like other jellyfish do, but they prefer not to.

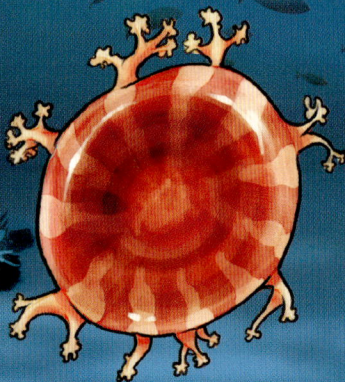

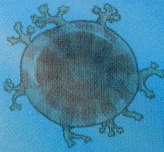

Their tentacles have dozens *(DUH-zenz)* of tiny mouths on them! They send sticky mucus *(MYOO-kus)* with stinging cells out into the water to stun, or shock, small plankton and fish. Then they gobble them up!

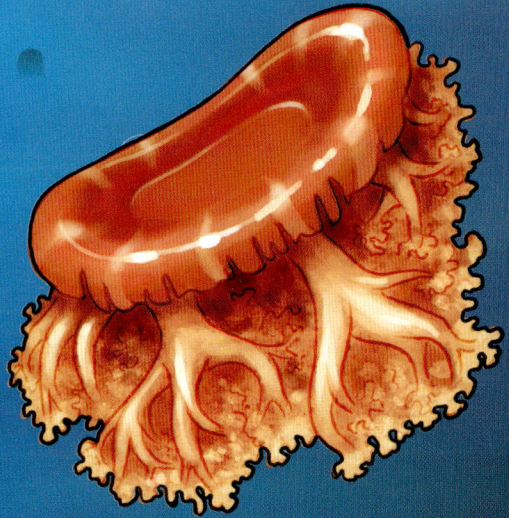

These jellyfish live in groups. Their tentacles look like flowers or seaweed waving in the ocean current when they are on the ocean floor.

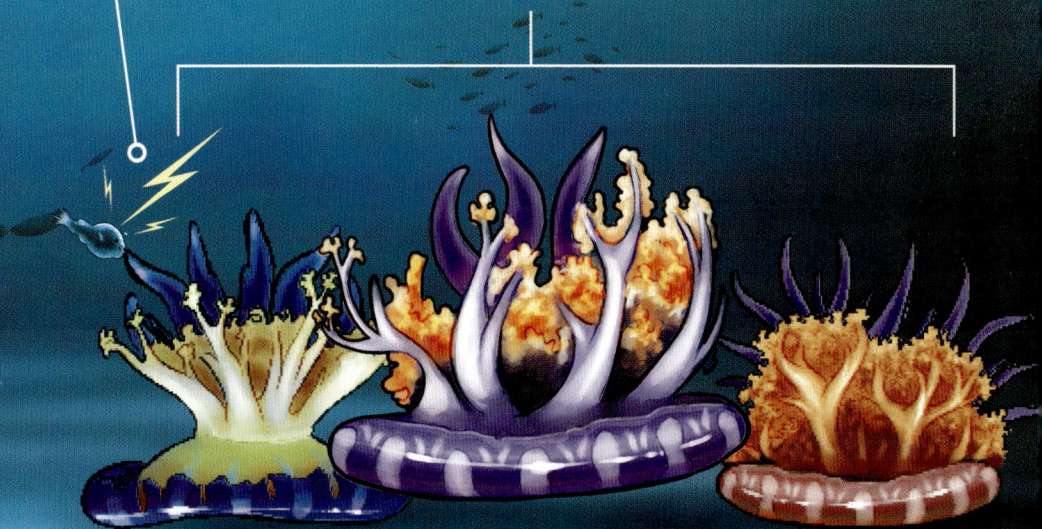

Vampire Bat

The only mammal that drinks the blood *(blud)* of other animals is the **vampire bat**! Vampire bats aren't picky. Any animal can provide them with blood.

Central America

South America

These nocturnal animals sleep in dark places like hollow *(HAH-loh)* trees or caves.

Vampire bats live in Central and South America. They live in colonies *(KAH-luh-neez)*, or groups, of a few to hundreds of bats.

nocturnal *(nok-TUR-nul)*: active *(AK-tiv)* or awake at night

When they bite, the venom *(VEN-um)* in their saliva *(suh-LY-vuh)* makes the blood of their prey flow faster.

Most bats only fly. Vampire bats fly, but they can also walk, run, and even jump!

Assassin Bug

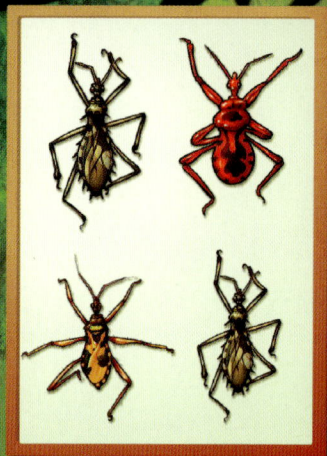

There are many species of **assassin** *(uh-SAS-in)* **bugs**. This bug has a long body, six legs, and a long mouth that looks like a drinking straw.

predatory *(PREH-duh-tor-ree)*: describes animals that eat other animals

They are predatory *(PREH-duh-tor-ree)* bugs that trap their prey. They hide, waiting for insects like caterpillars, flies, and other bugs to come along.

The assassin bug attacks its prey by piercing *(PEER-sing)* or poking a hole in it with its long mouth, then drinking the liquid from the insect's body.

Assassin bugs are venomous and will bite humans.

Dementor Wasp

Dementor *(duh-MEN-tur)* **wasps** are very small insects. They are red and black in color and live only in Thailand *(TY-land)*.

Thailand

They prey only on cockroaches. The dementor wasp will sting a cockroach and inject venom into its belly. This turns the cockroach into a "zombie" that cannot control its movement. Then, the dementor wasp guides *(gide-z)* the cockroach to the wasp's nest, pulling it by its antenna *(an-TEN-uh)*.

No one knows why the dementor wasps' venom causes *(KAW-zez)* this to happen!

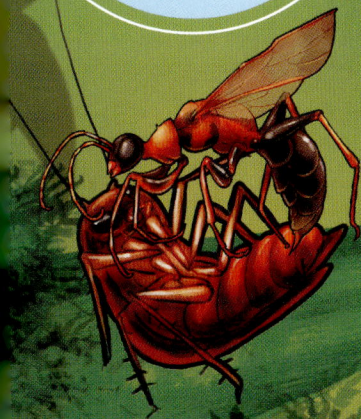

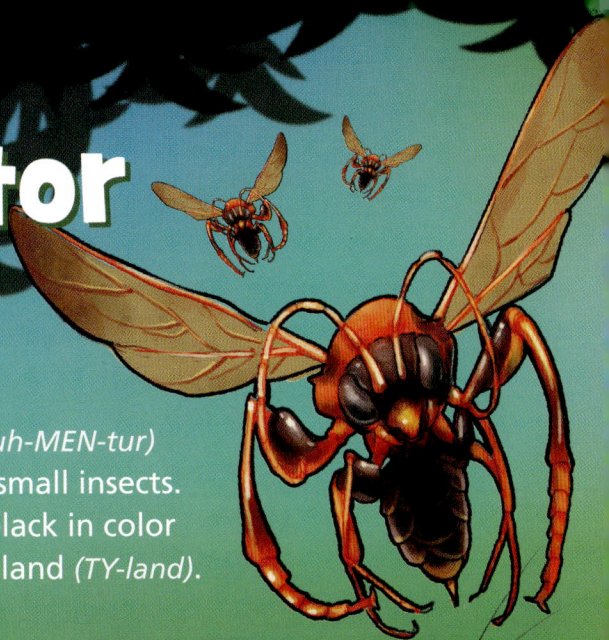

21

Flying Fox

The **flying fox** is really a type *(tipe)* of bat. It is called the flying fox because its face looks like a fox.

Flying foxes are nocturnal. They come out at night to eat fruit *(froot)* and pollen from flowers.

They live in large groups called camps. There can be over 10,000 bats in one area! They are very social *(SOH-shul)* animals.

5 ft

Flying foxes are the largest type of bat in the world! Their wingspan, or the distance from the tip of one wing to the other, can be 5 feet or longer.

Jerboa

The **jerboa** *(jur-BOH-uh)* is a very small and very fast type of mouse. Jerboas live in the hot, dry deserts *(DEZ-zurts)* of Africa *(AF-rih-kuh)* and Asia *(AY-zhuh)*.

They can run very quickly if they are being chased: up to 15 miles per hour!

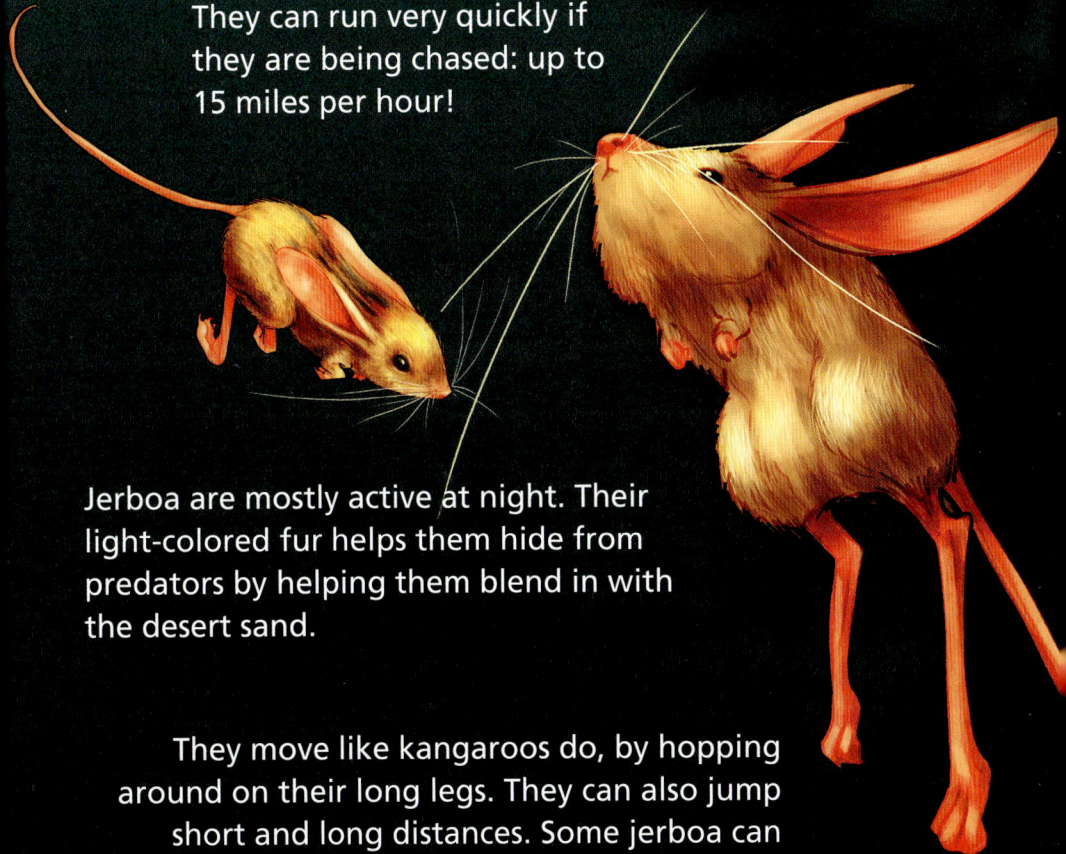

Jerboa are mostly active at night. Their light-colored fur helps them hide from predators by helping them blend in with the desert sand.

They move like kangaroos do, by hopping around on their long legs. They can also jump short and long distances. Some jerboa can jump up to 10 feet.

Pangolin

The **pangolin** *(PANG-goh-lin)* is the only mammal on Earth that is completely covered in scales. Their scales are made from keratin *(KEH-ruh-tin)*. This is the same material *(muh-TEER-ree-ul)* that human fingernails are made of!

If a pangolin is in danger, they roll themselves into a ball to protect *(proh-TEKT)* themselves.

Pangolins live in many different habitats in Africa and Asia.

Pangolins do not have any teeth.
They use their long snouts, or noses,
and tongues to eat insects.

They are very
shy animals and
mostly live alone.

One pangolin
can eat
70 million
insects each
year!

Naked Mole Rat

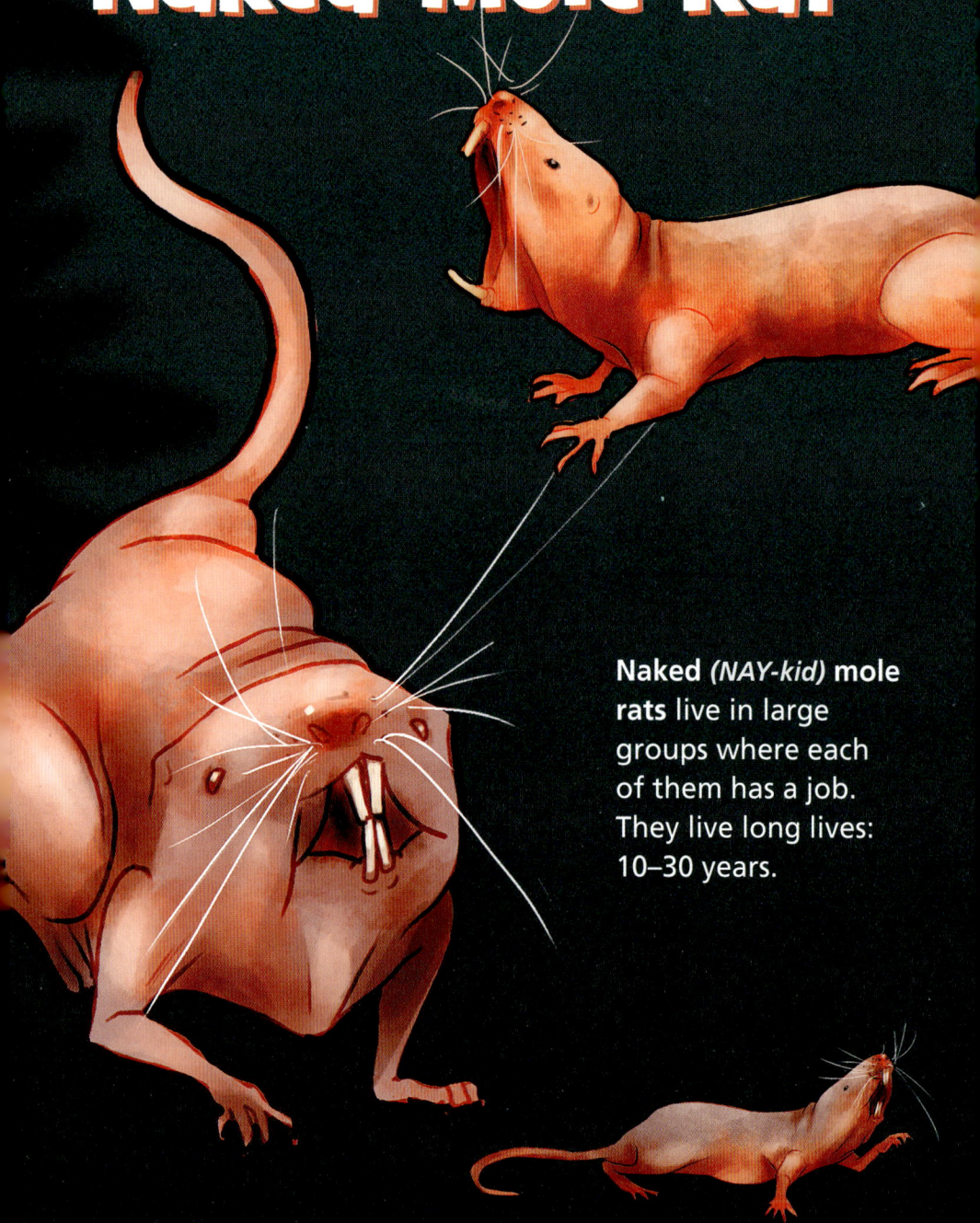

Naked (*NAY-kid*) **mole rats** live in large groups where each of them has a job. They live long lives: 10–30 years.

Naked mole rats are best known for the way they look. They are very small animals with large teeth and no hair.

They are mostly blind. They have around 100 whiskers *(WIS-kurs)* on their bodies that help them feel where they are and find their way around.

They live underground in tunnels that they dig using their teeth. These tunnels can be up to 6.5 feet deep and 2.5 miles long.

Raccoon Dogs

Raccoon dogs can climb trees! They are also the only type of "dog" that **hibernates** *(HY-bur-nayts)* during the winter.

hibernate *(HY-bur-nate)*: to sleep very deeply for a long time during winter

Raccoon dogs live in eastern Asia and parts of Europe *(YUR-up)*. They might look like raccoons, but they are more related to foxes and dogs.

They have thick fur that is usually *(YOO-zhoo-ul-lee)* black, gray, or brown. Their bodies are long, with short legs and claws on their feet. They live in forests, often in small groups with other raccoon dogs.

They are omnivores *(OM-nih-vorz)*, which means that they eat other animals and plants.

Superb Bird-of-Paradise

The **superb** *(suh-PURB)* **bird-of-paradise** *(PARE-uh-dise)* lives in the rainforests and mountains of New Guinea *(GIN-ee)*.

The male superb birds-of-paradise have dark black feathers. When they are trying to attract a female bird, they will move their feathers *(FEH-thurz)* to look like a cape around their heads.

New Guinea

They also have some bright blue feathers in the shape of a face across their chests. They show these feathers to the female and begin to hop around and do a funny "dance."

Blue-Footed Booby

Blue-footed boobies *(BOO-beez)* live on the coastline and islands *(I-lunds)* of the Pacific *(puh-SIF-ik)* Ocean.

They are best known for their bright blue feet. The blue color comes from the fish that they eat. The bluer the feet, the healthier *(HELTH-ee-ur)* the bird!

They are clumsy *(KLUM-zee)* on land, but they are graceful when flying in the air. They soar over the ocean and dive into the water at high speeds to catch fish.

Bee Humingbird

Bee hummingbirds are the smallest birds on Earth. They are between 2 and 2.5 inches long and weigh less than 0.1 ounce, about the same as a penny.

Some hummingbirds can fly for up to 20 hours without stopping. They can fly as fast as 30 miles per hour.

They use their long tongues to drink the nectar *(NEK-tur)* in flowers. They can visit up to 1,500 flowers a day.

They can fly upside down, backward, up, and down.

They live on the island of Cuba *(KYOO-buh)*. Their different colors help them blend into their habitats.

Riflebirds

Riflebirds *(RY-ful-burds)* live in rainforests in Australia *(aw-STRAYL-yuh)* and New Guinea *(GIN-ee)*. They are part of the bird-of-paradise family. They eat mainly insects, but they also eat fruit and seeds.

The riflebird got its name because the green-colored feathers on their chests look like uniforms *(YOO-nih-forms)* that the British Army wore in the 1700s.

They also have a call that sounds like a rifle *(RY-ful)* being fired. It is very loud!

They have curved beaks that they use to dig into tree limbs *(lims)* and under bark to find bugs.

New
Guinea

Australia

Burrowing Owl

The **burrowing** *(BUR-oh-ing)* **owl** is the only **raptor** to build nests underground. These owls live in North and South America in grasslands and deserts.

North America

South America

raptor: a large bird that eats small animals

Their brown and white feathers help them blend in easily *(EEZ-zih-lee)* with the ground where they live. They are small owls. Most adult burrowing owls are only 8–9 inches tall. Their wingspan reaches 20–24 inches.

They have long legs that they use to hop around. Unlike most owls, burrowing owls are active during the day.

Long-Wattled Umbrellabird

Long-wattled umbrellabirds
(long-WAH-tuld um-BREL-luh-burds)
live in South America.

This bird is named after the feathers
on top of its head that look like an
umbrella and the large **wattle** *(WAH-tul)*
that hangs off the male's chest. Only male
umbrella birds have large wattles.

wattle *(WAH-tul)*: a piece of skin that hangs off an animal's body

The wattle is covered in feathers. The wattle can be inflated *(in-FLAY-ted)*, or blown up like a balloon, when the male is trying to attract a female.

Long-wattled umbrellabirds eat mostly fruit. They can eat pieces of fruit whole.

GLOSSARY

algae *(AL-gee)*: tiny living things that make much of the Earth's oxygen *(OX-eh-jen)*

amphibian *(am-FIH-bee-un)*: an animal that has a backbone, or spine, and lives in water and on land

burrowing *(BUR-oh-ing)*: digging a tunnel or hole underground

colossal *(kuh-LAH-sul)*: very large

esca *(ES-cuh)*: an organ *(OR-gun)* on an animal that sticks out to attract other animals to it

desert *(DEH-zert)*: a hot, dry area where few plants grow and there is little rain

rainforest *(RAYN-for-est)*: a large forest that gets a lot of rain each year and has many types of plants and animals living in it

tropical *(TRAH-pih-kul)*: a humid *(HYOO-mid)* place with very warm temperatures *(TEM-pruh-churs)* all year long

venomous *(VEH-nuh-mus)*: a toxic substance *(SUB-stens)* that is harmful when injected into something

QUESTIONS TO THINK ABOUT

1. Which animal do you think was the the strangest? Why?

2. What is an interesting fact you learned about one of these animals?

3. Which animal(s) would you like to see in person? Explain your choice(s).

4. Which animal would you like to learn more about? What else would you like to know about this animal?

5. If you were to create a really strange animal, what kind of features would it have and why?

CODE READER™

Making Difficult Words Easy

Code Reader Books provide codes with "sound keys" to help read difficult words. For example, a word that may be challenging to read is "chameleon," so it might be followed by a code like this: chameleon *(kuh-MEE-lee-un)*.

The codes use phonetic keys for each sound in the word. Knowing the keys can help make reading the codes easier.

Code Reader™ Keys

Long a sound (as in make):
a *(with a silent e)*, **ai**, or **ay**
Examples: break *(brake)*;
area *(AIR-ee-uh)*; able *(AY-bul)*

Short a sound (as in cat): **a**
Example: practice *(PRAK-tis)*

Long e sound (as in keep): **ee**
Example: complete *(kum-PLEET)*

Short e sound (as in set): **e** or **eh**
Examples: metric *(MEH-trik)*; bread *(bred)*

Long i sound (as in by):
i *(with a silent e)* or **y**
Examples: might *(mite)*; bicycle *(BY-sih-kul)*

Short i sound (as in sit): **i** or **ih**
Examples: myth *(mith)*; condition *(kun-DIH-shun)*

Long o sound (as in hope):
o *(with a silent e)*, **oh**,
or **o** at the end of a syllable
Examples: molten *(MOLE-ten)*; ocean *(OH-shen)*;
nobody (NO-bah-dee)

Short o sound (as in top): **o** or **ah**
Examples: posture *(POS-chur)*; bother *(BAH-ther)*

Long u sound (as in cube): **yoo**
Example: unicorn *(YOO-nih-korn)*

Short u or schwa sound (as in cup): **u** or **uh**
Examples: pension *(PEN-shun)*; about *(uh-BOWT)*

Long oo sound (as in cool): **oo**
Example: school *(skool)*

Short oo sound (as in look): **o͝o**
Examples: wood *(wo͝od)*; could *(ko͝od)*

oy sound (as in boy): **oy**
Example: boisterous *(BOY-stur-us)*

ow sound (as in cow): **ow**
Example: discount *(DIS-kownt)*

aw sound (as in paw): **aw**
Example: faucet *(FAW-sit)*

qu sound (as in quit): **kw**
Example: question *(KWES-chun)*

zh sound (as in garage): **zh**
Example: fission *(FIH-zhun)*